Custody Coaching

Preparing For Battle

By:

R. Bruce Wallace

October 1, 2019
4700 N. Capital of Texas Hwy.
Ste. 220
Austin, TX. 78746
512-820-2745
info@custodycoaching.com
www.CustodyCoaching.com

www.CustodyCoaching.com

Table of Contents

ACKNOWLEDGEMENTS

I've had many influencers in my life. None greater than my God. This book is only possible because of His love, patience, direction and support. I knew He had a greater purpose for my life and it took me 22 years, since a car wreck that should have killed me, to figure it out.

I've learned if you stop and listen, He'll speak to you. If you ask God to shine a bright light on the path He has for your life, you'll see it. Once it's in plain sight, ask God for the strength, the courage and the faith you'll need to follow it; and, He'll help you. Thank you, Lord, for helping me with this book and all of the many blessings you've given me.

I'm extremely grateful for the unwavering love and support from my family and friends. However, my parents deserve special recognition. My parents have been married 65 years. They know what it takes to intimately love one another. They've done an amazing job teaching my brother, sister and me how to be parents. My mom and dad have always been there for me. Through thick and thin, good times and bad, my parents have always been by my side. They've done an amazing job of demonstrating what it means to have unconditional love for a child. Thanks, mom and dad.

You'd expect your family and friends to show up as witnesses to your custody trial and they certainly pulled through for me with flying colors. My custody trial was in San Antonio, Tx. This meant all of my witnesses had to come from out-of-town. One of my friends and business associates flew in from Nebraska. None of them gave it a second thought or expressed any concern for having to travel. They all wanted to be there to support Annabelle and me.

I have the deepest appreciation for Mary and Virginia. My sweet sister, Mary, took the stand and told beautiful and sincere stories of my life with Annabelle. My oldest nephew's wife, Virginia, who has spent many hours with Annabelle and me, recounted the fun times we'd all had together at parties and family socials. You two were awesome.

Angie drove all the way from Houston to voice her concerns for Annabelle due to her somewhat awkward socialization skills. Jeff flew all the way from Nebraska to share his observations of Annabelle and me together in Hawaii. He was passionate and sincere. And Teresa, as the Director of Engagement at Westlake Hills Presbyterian Church, was the first person we met when we visited and subsequently joined this wonderful church.

Teresa told stories of seeing Annabelle and me at church together. She talked about how genuinely excited Annabelle seemed when participating in Sunday School and the Children's Sermon on Sunday mornings. She acknowledged our regular attendance and desire to be involved with the church and its members. However; most importantly, she never swayed, during some very tough questions, with regards to her opinion of me as a good man, husband and father. Thank you, Teresa.

Amy Geistweidt and her staff, Dora and Bianca, put their heart and soul into my custody battle. They filtered through reams of material and isolated only those documents, pictures and videos that ultimately made a huge difference. Amy proved to not only be an amazing litigator; but, she's also an amazing strategist and tactician. There's no one better to help you with your divorce or custody issues than Amy. Today, she's more than my attorney, she's my friend.

And, there were other attorneys from the firm of Higdon, Hardy and Zuflacht who contributed to our success. This is an amazing family law firm with attorneys and staff who truly care for their clients. Thank you, HHZ.

My Manda, you're amazing! You are wise beyond your years and a truly dedicated wife, partner and mother. By the age of 31, you'd been through more than many women will ever experience in their lives. When we first started to become romantically involved, I warned you of my baggage and you were unphased. You're now my partner in business and I know you'll help many new step parents acclimate to their new and valuable family role.

You've stuck by my side and been totally loyal. You've taught me to love in ways I didn't know were possible. You've taught me how to fight fairly. And, with you, we're learning together the power of faith in our Father. You are my world and I love you BATS!

Sweet Annabelle, by the age of six, you've taught me more than you'll ever know. You are my first daughter. You came into this world two months early. You and I spent the first four days of your life in the NICU. I held you to my bare chest when you were barely bigger than the palm of my hand. We bonded instantly and have shared a special closeness ever since that moment.

You're a fighter, Annabelle. You're tougher than nails. You know when to push and you know when to stand down. You have an uncanny ability to transition back and forth between the life you have with your mother and the life you have with Amanda, Ruby and me. You've got me wrapped around your finger and that's just fine. Your daddy

loves you as Big As The Sky forever and always.

DEDICATION

To my girls: Amanda, Annabelle and Ruby

[CHAPTER 1] – WHY ME

Men win custody battles less than 8% of the time.

When I went into my third custody trial in Texas to

modify a Minnesota custody order, I was 60 years

old and 3 years into my 4th marriage and we'd just

had a baby. My daughter from my previous

marriage was 6 years old and my ex-wife (my

opponent) had had primary custody for the last

five years since our separation in 2013.

In March of 2015, we were both living in

Minnesota and my ex won full physical custody of

my daughter. I was given very unreasonable and unequal visitation access. And, the referee (In Minnesota, a referee is a judge in training.) granted my ex the right to move to Texas whenever she wanted.

Seventy-five days after the referee's ruling my ex took my daughter and moved to Texas. In order to maintain my minuscule visitation rights, I'd have to physically spend face-to-face time with my daughter at least once a month – regardless of her location. This meant many roundtrip flights from Minnesota to Texas. The order read that if I missed a single monthly face-to-face visit, for any reason, I'd lose all my visitation rights. The referee intentionally set me up to fail; and, my ex wanted and expected me to fail.

Within a year of the order I'd moved to Houston, Texas. I had to. I don't believe my ex ever expected I'd uproot my life and move from Minnesota. Our apartment in Houston was 225 miles from my daughter's home in San Antonio; and, my ex was determined to make it difficult for me to see my girl.

My ex wasn't compliant with our order. She forced me to go way out of my way for the exchanges. She was going to try anything to get me to give up and go away.

After my move to Texas, I was hopeful my ex would give me at least two weekends a month with my daughter. Not a chance. I'd eventually need legal help to get that done.

Now that we both lived in Texas, my first step was hiring a Texas attorney who would file the necessary documentation for Texas to take jurisdiction of my case. The second step was to set a hearing in Bexar County (San Antonio) for Texas to acknowledge and accept jurisdiction of my case. This would be my path for acquiring the Texas minimum Standard Possession Order for visitation. I won my first hearing and my time with my daughter increased exponentially.

There were a lot of factors which took place to push me further into a custody battle. My ex had demonstrated over the years, that as my daughter's primary care giver, she was physically, emotionally and financially neglectful. She was extremely controlling and made co-parenting a constant challenge.

I went into the custody trial past due over $50,000 in spousal maintenance (alimony), I owed her $60,000 in attorney's fees from our previous divorce and custody trial; and, I had been unemployed for 2 ½ years. A year and a half before the trial, my attorney had given me at best a 50% chance of winning full physical custody of my daughter. In fact, my attorney told me; "Bruce, you'd be better off reaching a visitation and financial settlement with your ex and take whatever you'll spend on attorney's fees going for custody and dedicate those dollars to Annabelle's college and wedding funds. I don't recommend we go for custody."

I took my attorney's advice and after several attempts to negotiate a settlement with my ex-wife, several court hearings on a variety of issues, mediation and fifteen months of my ex's flat refusal to negotiate on anything, I found myself in the Bexar County Courthouse in a full-blown and very contentious custody trial. Our case would be decided by a jury. Statistically, there's no way I should have won full custody, but I did.

So; why listen to or work with me? Because I've been there and done that. I doubt you've experienced, are experiencing or going to experience something I haven't already experienced in some form or fashion. You can learn from me. I can help you avoid making some of the same mistakes I made. You need to understand your rights and should get an unbiased opinion from someone who doesn't have a financial stake in your case. You need an experiential opinion regarding your chances of being awarded full custody.

Whether you're a mom or dad. Whether your divorce was amicable or heated. Whether you're considering going for full custody or modifying an existing order. You should seek the advice from an experienced coach whose only purpose is to make sure the best interests of your child are served.

Now, let's get started building your game plan.

NOTES

[CHAPTER 2] – A WINNING GAME PLAN

Preparing for a custody trial should be like prepping for the biggest sales presentation of your life. Think about it. You'll be trying to convince; or, in other words, sell a judge or jury to "buy" the fact that you're the best parent to have primary custody.

No one is a natural born salesperson. Selling is the *learned skill* of being able to understand your audience, disrupt their current mindset, identify their needs, provide reasonable solutions, overcome objections, ask for agreement and implement a mutually beneficial solution. If you're not approaching your custody battle with this skillset, you're leaving yourself at a distinct disadvantage.

A great way to organize your case as a sales presentation is building a SWOT (Strengths, Weaknesses, Opportunities and Threats) analysis. Your strengths and weaknesses are the internal factors of your case which you control. The opportunities and threats are the external forces at work and are mostly out of your control. To win, you should leverage your strengths and opportunities and avert your weaknesses and threats.

By clearly understanding and implementing strategies and tactics identified through your customized SWOT analysis you can expertly prepare for trial. I work closely with my clients and their attorneys to develop an individual SWOT analysis for their case. Then together, we build supporting strategies and tactics for each quadrant of your individualized SWOT greatly increasing your likelihood for success.

A SWOT Analysis is divided into personal/internal/controllable factors (Strengths and Weaknesses) and external/uncontrollable factors (Opportunities and Threats). The SWOT is also divided into areas we want to Leverage and areas we want to Avert. The following is a 3D image of how this works.

Custody SWOT Analysis

Wallace SWOT Blocks Overview

(Use the Appendix at the back of the book to begin building your SWOT.)

It's easy to see how organizing your case in this manner will give you a distinct advantage. Notice above in my model that the Leverage side clearly outweighs the Avert side. This is a good thing. A SWOT analysis with supporting strategies and tactics keeps you focused. You'll find yourself confidently able to leverage your Strengths and

Opportunities while averting the Weaknesses and Threats of your case.

Internal Factors are all items within your control. These are your individual strengths as a parent. This is your chance to identify what makes you the best parent for primary custody.

Are you a good co-parent? Are you financially secure? Are you an attentive parent? Do you look for ways to help improve your child's education and understanding of life? Do you have your child enrolled in extracurricular activities?

These are your Strengths and this is your chance to brag. Don't be shy. Carefully consider all the ways you're the right parent for primary custody. And, most importantly, consider strengths you can evidentially prove. You should have lots of pictures and videos of you doing these things with your child.

Be honest about your Weaknesses. Look in the mirror and layout all of the things your opponent will bring up that could portray you as the wrong person to have primary custody. The more of these you identify in advance the better prepared you'll be to attack these items when they're brought up in court. And, they will come up at trial. You can count on it.

The Opportunities and Threats are the external factors of your case. These are the things that are out of your control. However, just because they're out of your control doesn't mean you can't leverage the opportunities and avert attention away from the threats.

Opportunities are a way for you to focus on the weaknesses of your opponent's case. These must all be provable concerns you have for your opponent having primary custody. Note, I said provable. Don't list things you can't prove. Your opinions carry little weight at trial. Things you can prove carry a very heavy weight.

It's so easy to get caught up in the emotion of the trial. Your mind will race. You'll be angry. You'll be sad. You'll be upset over all the "lies" your opponent has told about you. You'll easily want to vent and throw them under the bus over any and everything. But don't! Take deep breaths and focus on only the things you can prove. This will give you immeasurable amounts of credibility with a judge or jury.

Your journal, videos and pictures are worth their weight in gold. Your opponent's bank and credit card statements with extravagant purchases and ignored utility bills are clear proof of their financial neglect of a child. Pictures of your child from FaceTimes living in filth or being ignored when they're sick will lend valuable credibility to your story. And, when opposing counsel tries to take you off track, you'll always have your SWOT map and the techniques to get back on track.

Threats are those aspects to your case that are out of your control and that you need to avert. You want to spend as little time as possible dealing with threats in front of the judge or jury. Having as many of these identified prior to trial gives you the ability to plan strategies and tactics to avoid them.

Examples of Threats:

- You're the father. Courts in the US aren't supposed to have a bias towards moms. Maybe your court won't. But, I clearly remember during jury selection, one of the jurors selected by opposing council said, "I'm going to vote for the mom. I feel daughters should be raised by mothers." There was nothing I could do about that. Being a dad is usually a disadvantage in a custody battle and it's out of your control. Don't get sucked in when opposing counsel has you on the stand and tries to get you to admit moms should be the natural care giver for children. You'll have prepared your SWOT and you'll know how to pivot back to your strengths.

- You're much older than the typical parent of a six-year-old. You'll want to build your case around the fact that your age doesn't matter. You're doing things with your child that younger parents do – biking, swimming, athletics, school, etc. Take age out of the equation and avert the conversation back to your strengths.

Identify as many threats as possible before trial. This will give you and your attorney lots of time to prepare a plan of action when they come up. The more you anticipate weaknesses and threats the better prepared you'll be to deal with them in court.

Each aspect of your individual SWOT requires detailed strategies and tactics to powerfully highlight your positives and successfully avert your negatives. It's important to utilize an experienced coach when building your strategies and tactics. If you've never done this before there's no reason to try and tackle this by yourself.

If you don't know how to sell or are uncomfortable selling, you'll need coaching. I've been in sales and marketing since I graduated Baylor University. I've had over 40 years of successful selling experience and I can teach you the intricacies of selling.

The most successful people I know are those who surround themselves with people who have skills that help them eliminate their individual areas of weakness. Think about your individual SWOT and contemplate the skills and types of people you'll need to be successful. With all of this in mind, you'll be able to put together a winning team and a winning game plan.

NOTES

[CHAPTER 3] – THE RIGHT ATTORNEY

Do you know the difference between a good attorney and a great attorney? A good attorney knows the law, but a great attorney knows the judge!

All kidding aside, I've had good attorneys and bad attorneys. I've had attorneys that fit my personality and ones that didn't. Nothing can be more detrimental to your case than having a bad attorney that's not a good fit for your personality.

People are always looking for the "best" attorney. However; not every attorney graduated at the top of their class. In fact, most attorneys graduated somewhere in the middle. So, stop looking for the "best" attorney in town and focus on making sure you have the *right* attorney for your personality and your case.

In my first divorce I had the right attorney. He knew what he was doing and our personalities clicked. He knew which direction to go and how to corner my soon to be ex-wife whom I'd caught having an affair with the Governor of Louisiana's nephew. For this reason, no one on her side wanted any publicity. My attorney leveraged this fact into a very effective and efficient divorce settlement. Everything went my way.

My second divorce experience was completely the opposite of my first. I was strapped for cash and went bargain shopping for an attorney. I eventually found an attorney who had been through a divorce himself and who I connected with instantly. We had good rapport and he *seemed right* for me. He was at the lower end of hourly attorney rates; and, he was easy to reach. (Today, both of these would be red flags for me.) If an attorney is too easy to reach and too cheap, it means they're probably not very good.

Early into the divorce I began to feel we were getting pushed around. We were usually late with responses. We never made similar discovery requests on my spouse. My attorney didn't fight or advocate for me the way a good attorney should.

A week before the divorce hearing my attorney called me to his office. I figured we were going to review my case and prepare for trial. Boy, was I wrong.

I sat across from him at his desk and he told me he was getting out of the family law business. He was tired of being an attorney and had taken a job to be a manager at a local hardware store. He was still planning to represent me at the hearing, but I'd need to find a new attorney for any work after the trial.

In court he was little to no help. He wasn't engaged. He didn't make any objections. He didn't try and pin my spouse down on any of her mistakes. It was a disaster.

The judge ruled totally in my spouse's favor. I got limited visitation. I had to pay all her attorney's fees. I had to pay a lot of alimony and the judge determined I'd have to pay almost double the maximum amount of child support allowed by statute in the state of Texas. This is what happens when you try to save money when shopping for an attorney.

There's no way I was going to let this happen in my third divorce. I filed for divorce in Minneapolis, MN. My soon to be ex had done lots of things wrong. There was a trail of lies, abuse and neglect. I thought I needed the best attorney money could buy.

I did my research, asked around and checked references. I found her. She had over 20 years of experience. She was feared in Minneapolis by a multitude of other divorce attorneys. She had a reputation of being a real tiger in court. I couldn't wait to meet her and get things going.

Ten minutes into our first meeting I knew our personalities did not click. We couldn't have been more different personally, politically or socially. One of her first questions to me was; "How much money do you make?" I told her; "I make a lot of money; and, I want to win this case." After finding out how much I made, she looked me straight in the eye and said; "You don't make a lot of money. That's peanuts compared to most of my clients."

At that moment I should have stood up and politely left the meeting. I should have never hired her. She might be a great attorney; but, knowing what I know today, there's no way she'd be the *right* attorney for me. However; based solely on her reputation, I swallowed my pride and hired her on the spot. Big mistake!

My spouse's attorneys asked for things over and over again: bank statements, credit card statements, frequent flyer accounts, employee benefits, 401k statements, deferred comp statements, tax returns and the demands went on and on. We asked for similar items but never to the point of demanding a thing. We acquiesced on almost all the discovery they failed to deliver and all along the way my attorney kept telling me; "Don't worry about it. When we get to trial, I'll nail them."

The child custody situation wasn't going to be easy. We both wanted full custody. I had to go for it because I knew in my heart of hearts my daughter would be better off with me. But my spouse and I were on opposite ends of the spectrum. No middle ground was going to work. We were ordered to get a child custody evaluation.

At first, this seemed like a good idea. I'd never been through a custody evaluation before. Surely a professional and neutral observer would do what I felt would be in the best interest of my daughter – give me full custody.

We were presented a list of highly regarded evaluators and my attorney told me any one of them would do a good job. We let my spouse's attorney choose and they went with Michael Goldfarb of Moxie, Inc. We set an introductory meeting at his office to get things started.

We both arrived on time and were escorted back to his office. There he was, an arrogant man with gigantic chips on his shoulders, perched in his swivel chair and ready to pounce. He was egotistical and abrupt. He'd found a career where he could have power and control over others; and, he loved his work.

Goldfarb opened our meeting by saying; "Your child custody process is going to be brutal. You're going to have to disclose things you'd never disclose to anyone. You're going to say dreadful and mean things about each other. You're not going to like me at all. And; if you two think you don't like each other today, wait until we get done with this process. By then, you'll really hate each other."

My jaw must have hit the floor. Wait, what!?!? This is going to be our starting point for my child custody evaluation? Who in their right mind would sign up for this process with this guy? I was confused and immediately put on guard.

My ex and I listened as he gave us instructions. You could have cut the air with a knife. Interestingly, my spouse seemed to be getting along pretty well with him. They actually exchanged a few smiles. My spouse was being a little flirtatious and Goldfarb was eating it up. I was in trouble.

After the meeting I called my attorney and told her what I'd experienced and thought we should immediately get a different custody evaluator. My attorney dismissed my concerns and told me she'd worked with Goldfarb with several of her clients and there'd never been a problem. She assured me we'd be fine.

Goldfarb was right. He was miserable. I didn't like him or his process one bit. He was rude and condescending. He was never accommodating and clearly didn't like me. At every opportunity he pitted my spouse and I against each other. He set up his ONE announced visitation to both our homes and spent no more than two hours observing each of us with our daughter. He gathered all of the forms from us that he had asked us to fill out and went to work on his recommendation. Needless to say, it didn't go well for me.

I lost everything. EVERYTHING! In a day and age where most evaluators feel it's in the child's best interest to have both parents actively involved in the child's life, Goldfarb recommended my spouse be able to take our child and move back to

Texas. He didn't think my involvement as a father was necessary for our daughter to have a healthy upbringing. He even referred to my spouse as being feisty, in a positive manner. He was playing cute with my spouse in his evaluation summary. I was appalled.

My attorney was shocked by his evaluation and we went into full fight mode. We hired the nation's leading expert on custody evaluation. He was from Pennsylvania. He was past president of the Professional Academy of Custody Evaluators. We asked him to review the evaluation and possibly testify at my trial.

He went through Goldfarb's entire evaluation and came back to us feeling we could get Goldfarb's evaluation dismissed. He pointed out numerous examples of Goldfarb's bias towards my wife. He documented numerous lies my wife had made. He went into great detail that we wouldn't be able to use the results of my wife's psychological exam because she'd been so dishonest with her answers. The tests' results were unreliable. My expert's analysis and testimony were going to save the day.

We flew him in for trial. He was well credentialed, well-spoken and confident on the stand. He set everything up perfectly for our cross examination of Goldfarb. He was brilliant.

Goldfarb was admittedly caught having made mistakes. He admitted he had not been entirely professional in his descriptions of my wife. He admitted to not necessarily being consistent and most importantly that he had a "slight" bias towards my wife. Bingo. I felt there was no way the referee could put any weight on Goldfarb's evaluation. Goldfarb is a greedy and horrible child custody evaluator.

When it came time for my attorney to cross examine my wife, my attorney was at best somewhat disorganized. It seemed as though all of our trial prep had gone out the window. My attorney was intimidated by my wife. The only tiger in the courtroom was my ex!

Where was the tiger I thought I'd hired? The main thing my attorney decided to focus on to demonstrate my wife wouldn't be a fit parent for primary custody, was her obsession for fast food. Stupid.

My attorney went through bank statement after bank statement pointing out that my wife had been to McDonald's or Dairy Queen. It became boring and silly. My wife admitted she liked Diet Coke from McDonald's and went there often. The fast food attack was a disaster.

Clearly, my extremely credentialed attorney had put little or no effort into my case prep. She was out maneuvered and out matched by opposing counsel. At some point, she had decided I wasn't worth the effort. I was extremely disappointed with her representation.

The referee issued her order fully following Goldfarb's recommendation. My now ex-spouse could leave Minnesota and move back to Texas whenever she was ready. I was given a very restrictive visitation schedule and had to pay an exorbitant amount of alimony and child support.

Looking back, I don't think I hired a bad attorney. I believe she's probably a good attorney for the right client. However; without any doubt, I know I hired the wrong attorney for me. The worst part about this admission is, I knew it from the start and chose her anyway.

On a side note, I was somewhat vindicated a couple of years later. I owed her more than $80,000. I didn't feel she'd earned it and I offered her what I felt was a reasonable settlement. She ended up suing me for 100% of her attorney's fees. I hired a *good and right* attorney for less than $1,000 and ended up not having to pay her a dime. YESSSS!!!

I moved to Texas at my earliest convenience to be closer to my daughter. My ex was being extremely controlling and unreasonable with regards to visitation. My only recourse would be to hire another attorney and seek a modification to the existing order. Up to this point, for my divorces, I'd hired one right attorney, one bad attorney and one wrong attorney. I needed a good attorney that would be the right attorney for me and my case which would now be in San Antonio, TX.

I did extensive research with regards to the type of representation I'd need. I knew I'd need an attorney who was a working mom with lots of experience. I needed the empathy this would provide. Male attorneys can come across as bullies when pitted against a single working mom.

I wanted an attorney whose only practice was family law. I wanted an attorney who was part of a successful family law practice surrounded by other experienced family law attorneys. This was important because in a good family law firm, attorneys bounce ideas off of one another. In this way, you hire one attorney but have access to several. And, most importantly, my attorney would need to mesh well with my personality.

Having a good attorney who was right for me made all the difference in the world. She was always well prepared. She was aggressive without coming across as a bully. We never missed a deadline. She was constantly thinking strategically and tactically. She took a genuine interest in my new spouse and me. But, maybe most importantly, I could tell from the get go that she really cared about my daughter. She believed everything I told her and deeply felt my daughter would be better off with me.

I learned that when your attorney is as passionate about your success as you are, your chances for success increase exponentially. I found the *right* attorney for my battle and the results of

my last trial speaks for itself.

NOTES

[CHAPTER 4] – IN THEIR BEST INTEREST

"Is it in the child's best interest?" You'll hear this question over and over as you start down the path of a custody battle. The attorneys and judges will use this question constantly. This is the standard for determining who will have primary custody of a child. This must be the foundation of your thought process as you begin to determine if you should even consider a custody battle. But sometimes, egos get in the way.

It's an unfortunate fact that many couples divorcing look for ways to exert power and control over each other. As an example, throughout the divorce and child custody process, the breadwinner might use money to exert power and control and the primary caregiver might use custody of the child(ren) to exert power and control. When this happens, the best interests of the child are lost.

Divorce, even the most amicable ones, involve hurt feelings. Couples have to carefully navigate the divorce/custody process trying to always remain sensitive to each other's feelings. When feelings get hurt and emotions run hot, the logical process gets thrown out the window.

All courts should base child custody decisions on the best interests of the child standard. This means the judge or jury should determine the custody arrangement that best suits the child's needs based on a variety of factors. Since every state addresses child custody cases slightly differently the factors that the judge or jury considers will vary slightly depending on the state in which the case is filed.

Generally; and for most states, the primary factors a judge or jury considers when determining the best interest of a child aren't limited to but will likely include:

- **Evidence of parenting ability**. Courts look for evidence that the parent requesting custody is genuinely able to meet the child's physical, emotional and financial needs. This includes food, shelter, clothing, medical care, education, loving support, and general parental guidance. Courts also consider the parents' physical and mental health when deciding a custody arrangement that would be in the child's best interest.

- **Consistency**. When considering a change, the courts try to determine how that change would affect the child. Courts generally prefer to keep kids' routines consistent. This includes living arrangements, school, child care routines, and access to extended family members. When possible, family court judges and juries prefer not to disrupt a child's routine.

- **The child's age**. Children under the age of five generally need more hands-on care than older children. Courts also look at the bond between the child and each of the parents when evaluating child custody options and deciding what would be in the child's best interests. In addition, when children are young, judges and juries frequently defer to the parent who has been the primary caregiver in the child's life. Some courts will also consider the child's wishes, depending on their age, generally twelve years and older.

- **Safety**. This factor is always top of mind in family court, and judges and juries will readily deny custody to a parent if they believe the child's safety would be compromised.

The court is looking at your child holistically. The court is considering safety, age, consistency and parenting skills. In general, when determining custody, courts aim to ensure both parents have the opportunity to be an active part of the child's life.

You <u>might</u> be, not <u>will</u> be, <u>might</u> be awarded primary custody if and only if you can prove: *The circumstances of the child; or, a person affected by the standing order, have materially and substantially changed to the point of having an extremely negative effect on the best interests of the child.* In other words, the parent with primary custody and/or that parent's circumstances have to have changed so much that they are no longer able to satisfactorily meet the minimum standards for caring for the child.

So; as you begin to consider full custody, constantly ask yourself this very important question: *"Is my having full custody of (insert child's name) in his/her/their best interest?"*

If you can't confidently answer yes to this question then perhaps you should consider other options. If you know you should have full custody then you need a plan. You should build your case strategically with supporting tactics which allow you to leverage the strengths and opportunities and avert the weaknesses and threats of your case.

NOTES

[CHAPTER 5] – PREPARING FOR AND BEING AT TRIAL

Believe it or not, preparing for a custody trial began the moment you decided to have a child. Your actions, the way you parent, the decisions you make and how you live your life all have consequences regarding your success should you ever need to go for custody. Every record of every event involving you with your child from the day your child is born will either help or hurt your case.

You have to document everything. And, I mean everything. I started out using a spiral bound day planner to keep track of times, places and events. This worked but it meant all my pictures and videos were kept in different files on my computer that were separate from my journal. It was cumbersome and I felt disorganized.

My journaling got much simpler and more organized once I downloaded and started using the Day One app. This is an excellent electronic journal for keeping up with your thoughts, locations and pictures. This app also allows you to print beautiful books that creatively tell your parenting story.

You need to keep track of every encounter you have with your child. This means documenting how much time you spent on the phone with your child and what you talked about. It means logging every exchange with your ex. It means taking pictures when you're with your child and logging them daily. Remember, you want pictures and videos of your daily routines not just the "Disney" moments. You can't over document your time with your child.

Because divorce and custody battles can be highly confrontational, we tend to look for all the ways our ex is screwing up. We think it's in our best interest and work hard to document all the mistakes the other person makes. Judges and juries get disinterested if you continually throw your ex under the bus. Document the bigger mistakes your ex makes and let all the trivial items slide. Spouse bashing fatigue will set in with the judge or jury and hurt your case. Instead, focus on lots of positive examples of you with your child.

Judges and juries enjoy seeing you have a positive role in your child's life. Happy videos and pictures demonstrating you're a hip parent will go a long way towards convincing the jury you're the right parent for primary custody. Pictures and videos are worth thousands of words. Showing yourself as a good parent subconsciously plants a seed with the court that you're also likely to be an agreeable and reasonable co-parent.

When you're on the stand, look at the person talking to you. Offer them the same professional courtesy you'd offer people that work with you. This means looking at the appropriate attorney or the judge when they ask you a question. An occasional glance away from the person asking you the questions and towards the judge or jury is appropriate when emphasis is needed. But, for the most part, stay engaged with the person talking to you.

Your actions off the stand are just as important as your actions on the stand. The judge and jury are always looking at how you react to what's being said about you. If your spouse is on the stand and you know they're lying (and they will) you can't react by shaking your head, banging your fist, sighing or rolling your eyes. This is perceived as a huge negative by judges and juries.

When you hear one of your witnesses say something you agree with, don't nod your head up and down. This looks like your coaching or leading the witness. You need to maintain a calm and neutral demeanor.

Your actions speak volumes. Non-verbal communication can be deafening. The looks you make and your actions can negatively affect your chances of winning without you even opening your mouth to speak.

Judges and juries are constantly looking for reasons to like or believe one spouse over the other. You don't want to give them any reasons to dislike you. You need and want them to have lots of positive thoughts about you, your ability to co-parent and the way you parent your child.

NOTES

[CHAPTER 6] – APPEARANCE MATTERS

It's a terrible misconception to believe the only time a judge or jury is watching you is when you're on the stand. They've got their eyes on you the moment either you or they walk into the courtroom. The judge is checking you out from the beginning of the trial. The prospective jurors are drawing conclusions about you as they're being marched in for voir dire.

Once judges and jurors know who you are, they'll be watching you and drawing conclusions about you even when you're outside the courtroom. They're looking at you and making judgements about you. Therefore; since we know this to be true, we should use it to our advantage.

Dress and look the part. If you're a professional, sophisticated, single, working mom then look the part. Don't overdo your makeup. Don't show up in high, strappy heels, long sharp fingernails and dangly earrings. If you look like you're ready to go to the local nightclub then you don't look like you're ready to be a parent. Slacks, a nice blouse and maybe a sweater look nice. Don't wear a lot of jewelry. Do wear a strand of pearls if you have them. Judges and juries see pearls as innocence and sophistication. This is a nice compliment to your overall look.

Men, don't go to trial looking like anything other than a hip, energetic and enthusiastic dad. This means you want to wear slacks, a nice button-down shirt (open collar, no tie) and a sport coat. Nothing else will do. Your hair should be clean and neat. If you have facial hair, consider losing it. People think men with beards or mustaches have something to hide.

Now that we have you looking the part, remember to act the part. Politeness and giving others professional courtesy matter. Be yourself, don't act. This isn't a performance and a savvy judge will see right through you.

Consider that the judge or jury are always looking for as many reasons as possible to determine if you are the best parent for primary custody. They're looking for things to like about you and things to dislike about you. Make sure your

courtroom actions and appearance present as

many reasons as possible to paint you as the best

parent for primary custody.

NOTES

[CHAPTER 7] – THE TRUTH DOESN'T HAVE TO

ANSWER THE QUESTION

You've heard it your whole life and now you're

hearing it from me. Tell the truth. When you've lied

in the past you know how difficult it was to keep

everything straight. Your custody battle and

divorce are difficult enough. If you're constantly

having to cover your tracks and keep your story

straight it will be exhausting. Telling the truth

simplifies your case and greatly increases your

chance for success.

However, did you know you can tell the truth but not necessarily answer the question you're being asked? This requires practice and strategic listening combined with carefully considered answers. Learning this technique can keep you from exposing weaknesses in your case.

At trial, opposing counsel might ask you; "How much money do you make?" One answer, a truthful answer, could be the total amount of gross income you declared on your most recent tax return. Answering the question this way would be divulging your entire income from all sources. But that wasn't the question. The question was; "How much money do you make?"

If you're trying to avoid divulging your total gross income, which is let's say $250,000, you could truthfully answer the question saying; "My salary is

$100,000." Then, you shut up and wait to see what the attorney does with that information. A smart attorney might ask a follow-up question like; "Is that your total income from all sources?" However, many attorneys will hear your salary answer and move on to the next topic. Which is exactly what you want them to do. You never had to talk about your side gig or the bonuses you received because you told the truth about your salary.

Perhaps you get asked, "Are you behind on alimony payments?" You could answer; "I've paid over $150,000 in alimony." Or, "I've never been late or missed a child support payment." Both answers are true. They both highlight the strengths of your case yet neither answers the question you were asked. The judge and/or jury hear the positive and the attorney might just move on. At a minimum, you've diverted a weakness of your case and

turned it into a positive.

So; remember, don't lie. Listen carefully.

Ponder the question and carefully formulate your

answer. You can tell the truth, highlight the

strengths of your case, avert your weaknesses and

throw the other side off balance by responding

with truthful answers that don't necessarily answer

the question you're asked.

NOTES

[CHAPTER 8] – THE HIGH ROAD

Human nature pushes us to defend our position. We want to believe we're always right and it's difficult to admit when we're wrong. However; having a mindset of always having to be right going into a divorce and child custody battle is terribly non-productive.

First of all, we all know we aren't always right. More importantly, we don't always have to be right all the time to win the battle. In fact, if you want to keep the lines of communication open it's important along the way to concede to your spouse's position.

Taking the high road requires discipline, effort and practice. It's all about humility. It's treating others the way you'd want them to treat you.

I owned a home in Minnesota and all of my business contacts were in Minnesota. This was important because I was looking for a job. The referee knew I couldn't just pick up and move. I made sure the referee knew I had family in Houston and that I'd need to go there to visit my daughter. With this in mind the referee ordered that my ex would have to drop off and pick up my daughter in Houston on the weekends that I came to Texas.

When my ex left Minnesota she moved to

San Antonio, Texas. Her home in San Antonio was

225 miles from my family's home in Houston and a

4 ½ to 6-hour drive depending on traffic. Having

my ex drop off and pick up my daughter in

Houston lasted about 4 months.

It was the fifth month and I'd made plans to

come to Houston for my visit with my daughter. This

meant I had coordinated with my parents to be

able to stay with them and borrow their car; and,

I'd used my frequent flyer miles to book and pay

for my non-refundable airline tickets. My next

opportunity to take the high road was just around

the corner.

My ex sent me a text and told me she

wouldn't bring my daughter to Houston for my

upcoming visit. I asked why and she told me she

just couldn't do it. She never gave a reason because I'm sure she didn't have one. She was just tired of making the long round trip to Houston.

I could have involved my attorney. I could have tried to get a judge to enforce the order and make my ex drive to Houston. I could have gotten in a big fight with my ex. I could have called her names and involved the authorities. But, I didn't.

I took a deep breath and offered to meet my ex half way between Houston and San Antonio. We met in a small town called Schulenburg. Miraculously, whatever had been keeping my ex from making the exchange in Houston vanished. The visitation was back on track and the best interests of my daughter were served.

It's called the high road for good reasons. The path is usually more challenging and more difficult. The high road is typically the more demanding and inconvenient path; but, in my life, the high road has always been the least congested and most scenic route. Take the high road.

NOTES

[CHAPTER 9] – THE TOASTER

A mentor once told me:

"Fight battles big enough to matter and small

enough to win."

Ed Dewees

How many times do we find ourselves in trivial

arguments in the <u>healthy</u> relationships we have

today? We eventually work through these and

rarely do they escalate out of control. However;

when you're in the middle of a challenging divorce

or custody battle, mole hills become mountains.

In my divorce we'd gotten to the point where we were dividing property. We powered through all the things we each brought into the marriage with only a few disagreements. And, for some reason, most of the really big items we bought together were easy to divide.

As we worked through the smaller things we'd purchased together, tensions began to rise. And then one day, all hell broke loose. We fought over this, that and the other and then we came to what must have been an extremely valuable and sentimental item – the toaster. Oh my god. The toaster!

We went around and around in a texting conversation. "I bought it because I like toast done a certain way!" "I paid for it. It's mine!" "You don't even like toast!" We both threatened to involve our attorneys – over the toaster. Things quickly spun out of control and far beyond reason.

There's no question there are times you need to take a stand. There will be principles, events and things that require your advocacy. You might be able to bend but you won't be able to break. In these moments; and for these things, stand your ground.

At this time in your life, the emotions are always bubbling just below the surface. It doesn't take much to let go and let it fly. After all, you're likely hurt and angry. You have to do your best to maintain perspective and it's not always easy.

I don't know what happened; but, I stopped. I took a breath. I started scrolling back through the text messages about the toaster. That's when I decided to pour myself a scotch, began to laugh and gained some perspective. I was fighting over a toaster! I wasted time, energy and emotion over a fricken toaster. It would have been considerably easier to right away let the damn thing go. I don't think I ever used it again.

Sometimes our egos get in the way and this makes things very difficult. Human nature pushes us to always defend our position. We want to believe we're always right and it's difficult to admit when we're wrong.

Let the toasters go!

NOTES

[CHAPTER 10] – NEVER INVOLVE YOUR CHILD

Even if you do everything right, your divorce and/or child custody battle will put your child(ren) through one of the most traumatic events of their life. And, you won't do everything right. You're going to make mistakes.

Perhaps the biggest mistake some parents make is putting the child in a position to have to choose one parent over another. Any parent who thinks this is a good idea will be in for a rude awakening as the child matures. In the end, parents who pit their child against their ex will ultimately lose their child's respect.

My daughter and I had been on the road together just over two hours after an exchange in Schulenburg and we were pulling into the apartment complex in Houston where we lived. My four-year-old daughter and I had had a fun drive. She'd taken a nap, had a snack, we'd played I spy, sang songs and thoroughly enjoyed each other's company. We pulled into a parking spot and before I could get out of the car, I heard my daughter's soft voice ask, "Daddy, why don't you want me?"

Whoa! I instantly knew her mother had put that thought in her head; but, I asked anyway, "Sweetheart, why are you asking me that?" Without hesitation she said, "Mommy told me you don't want me."

Tears welled up in my eyes as I tried to keep it together. I explained to my daughter I'd loved her before she was born and have always wanted and needed her in my life. I went around to her door, took her from her car seat and held her in my arms. I made sure she knew – without any doubt – that she was the center of my universe and I would love her forever. I'd always needed and wanted her in my life.

It would have been easy to throw her mother under the bus; but, that's not what needed to happen. The most important thing I could do was unwind the damage her mother had done. It was important my daughter knew I unconditionally loved and cared for her.

On another occasion, my daughter was with me for our extended summer visit. At dinner, she asked me, "Why don't you give mommy any money?" What?!?! At this point I'd given her mom hundreds of thousands of dollars. I was paying child support every month and doing my best to repay past due alimony. But I wasn't shocked to be getting this question.

I told my daughter the truth, which never gets you in trouble. I explained to her that I'd given her mom lots of money and that I always give her mom money every month. I explained that a month had never gone by that I hadn't given her mom money so she'd always be able to take care of her.

My daughter looked at me and said, "Then why can't mommy and I go to the park?" "What, Honey? What do you mean you can't go to the park?" "Every time I ask mommy if we can go to the park, she tells me we can't because the park costs money and daddy doesn't give us any money. Mommy tells me it's your fault we can't go to the park."

I asked my daughter when we're together had she ever seen us have to pay money to go to the park. She said, "No." I asked if any of the things we did at the park needed money to work. She said, "No." We talked about how using the swings and slides were free to anyone who wants to use them and I explained this is how it worked in San Antonio too. She got it and quickly moved the conversation to Barbie dolls. If you don't know it all ready, I'm here to tell you, kids remember everything!

Later that week, I put my daughter on a FaceTime with her mom. After a few casual hellos from each other my daughter said, "Why are you so mean to daddy?" My ex stuttered and tried to gather her thoughts. She said, "I, I, I don't say mean things about your daddy."

My four-year-old daughter now visibly angry cut her mom short, "Yes you do. You say he's cheap and he doesn't give us any money. Daddy's not cheap!"

Her mom jumped in and said, "I don't call him cheap." My daughter followed up with, "You tell me daddy doesn't give us any money. Daddy gives us money every month. And, we don't need money to go to the park!"

My ex quickly changed the subject but the damage was done. Her credibility was shot. Lies exposed. Love lost. And, as my daughter gets older and the lies continue the consequences will only get worse.

In most circumstances, your children need both of their parents in their lives. They don't want to have to choose between mom and dad; and, you should never put them in the position of having to make a choice. If you have a problem with your ex, take it to your ex. Don't go through your children to make a point. You'll drive a wedge between you and your child which you may never be able to remove.

NOTES

[CHAPTER 11] – BE CAREFUL PLAYING THE VICTIM

It seems today more and more people claim to be victims when in fact they're just experiencing the consequences of their own poor choices. For some, the victim card is easily played when in fact there isn't a victim. This doesn't sit well with judges or juries.

However, to be clear, some people really are victimized. Some people are on the receiving end of some tragic and horrible events. There are legitimate circumstances which could make you a victim. Under these circumstances, be loud and clear with your story.

Specifically, with divorce and child custody, there are absolutely times when a spouse or child is the victim of some very abusive spousal behavior. When this happens, judges and juries will want to see; and, should see evidence of the abuse. In these situations, custody decisions become matter of fact.

However, Judges and juries are put off by victimless victims. Judges and juries are looking for strong, independent and capable parents. They're looking for the parent who owns up to their mistakes, demonstrates they've learned from them and accepts responsibility for their actions. You'll find little sympathy from judges and juries if your testimony attempts to put blame for your shortcomings and poor decisions on your spouse.

In my trial, I couldn't help but notice that every time my spouse tried to blame me for her problems, I'd see jurors roll their eyes or disconnect from what was being said. Unlike a criminal trial where victims are attacked beyond their control, divorce/custody trials primarily exist due to the choices made by each spouse. So, accepting responsibility for your actions and circumstances goes a long way towards building your credibility, maturity and independence for being the primary care giver for your child.

My ex's case was totally built around finances. She was determined to prove that because I was behind on alimony, I was a bad parent and provider; and, more importantly, because I was behind on alimony my ex was unable to be a caring, attentive and nurturing parent. Not having enough money got in the way of everything she wanted to do for our daughter.

What she couldn't wrap her arms around was the fact that she'd been given hundreds of thousands of dollars and had nothing to show for it. I'd already paid her in alimony, child support and property settlements more money than some of the jurors would make in 10 years! There were examples, month after month of her having deposits of over $10,000 with her getting her nails and hair done. In those same months she went clubbing and out to dinner with friends. She bought cigarettes and went to the liquor store. She spent hundreds of dollars on makeup and clothing.

And yet, in those same months, the electricity got turned off because the bill hadn't been paid. Or, she chose not to make her car payment. She claimed she didn't have enough money to have our daughter in pre-school. She didn't have enough money to put her in gymnastics, dance, tennis or cheerleading.

There was no way a jury was going to see her as a financial victim. And, the harder she tried the more disconnected the jury became. Money had nothing to do with her ability to provide for our daughter. Misplaced priorities and selfishness had everything to do with the neglect my daughter experienced.

Unless you were seriously victimized be careful not to play the victim.

NOTES

[CHAPTER 12] – MONEY

It wasn't until I thought I was ready to publish my book when I realized I hadn't even talked about money. What was I thinking? How can you prepare for battle and not think about the financial implications of getting divorced or going for full custody? Then it dawned on me. As I prepared for my custody battle, finances were the least of my concerns.

Now, don't misunderstand me. I'm not now, nor have I ever been independently wealthy. In fact, I'd say my personal financial situation is quite the opposite. When I began preparing for my custody battle, I was already over $250,000 in debt and the debt was growing. I'm still paying off my battle today.

But, my conviction, my deep-down gut feeling, was that I knew I had to do what would be best for my daughter – regardless of the cost. Wow! When that's truly how you feel you begin to understand just how seriously you've taken your role in your child's life.

So, how do you financially prepare for a custody battle?

Honestly, I'm probably not the best person to answer this question. But, I do know this. When you get married and you and your spouse sit down to map out your household budget and finances, divorce and custody battles are not line items in your spreadsheet. Can you imagine the look on your newlywed's face if you said, "Okay Honey. It looks like we've covered just about everything. However, I think we better add a couple more line items and start setting money aside for our possible divorce and custody battles down the road." Yep, just mentioning that would probably get your marriage off on the wrong foot.

However, just as I said earlier in this book, the moment you decide to have a child is the moment you should begin to prepare for your custody battle. Likewise, you need to consider that finances should be part of your preparation. Whether you handle this in a pre-nup or accept the possibility that part of your future savings might be used for a divorce, you need to be prepared.

Getting divorced and/or going for custody is expensive. Even if you're planning an amicable split, it's going to cost more than you think. If it's a contentious split and you're headed for trial, you might as well take a deep breath knowing you're about to spend six figures to settle the battle. And, if you think winning the court battle means you're off the hook, you're wrong.

The judge or jury might award you full custody and rule that your now ex is fully responsible for the total cost of your legal fees. But, this means you have to be able to collect the money from your ex. Your attorney is going to look to you to get paid. They're not going to expect your ex is going to write them a check. So, it's going to be extremely expensive and it's going to be your responsibility to pay your legal fees.

Once you know you're in for a divorce and/or custody battle, lock down your finances. Step back and cut back on all your normal spending. Begin to prepare financially for the worst possible scenario.

It will help if you never lose sight of why your pursuing full custody. Keep pictures of your child all around your home. Pray for your child every day. Ask God to give you the finances, strength and courage you'll need to do what you know is in your child's best interest.

You'll peacefully know you're absolutely doing the right thing personally and financially if you can look in the mirror every day and confidently say to yourself, "I'm doing this because I know in my heart of hearts my child needs me more today than ever before. And, I know my child will need me more in the future than she needs me

today." Truly, peace will come and things will work

out. Give it to God and never look back.

NOTES

[CHAPTER 13] – IN THE END

As difficult as this may be to accept, you have to remember a custody battle isn't about winning or losing to your ex. You shouldn't be going for full custody to harm your ex. Custody battles are not about exerting power or authority over each other.

A custody battle should only occur when the best interests of the child aren't being met and/or the parents can't agree on the terms of access to the child. That's it. If you're in it for any other reason, you're wasting your time, energy, money and emotions.

Once you've determined the best interests of the child aren't being met and you realize you have to go to battle, keep these 11 things in mind:

1. Have a winning game plan.

2. Hire the *right* attorney for you and your circumstances.

3. Be certain what you're doing is in the best interests of the child.

4. You can't over prepare for trial.

5. The way you look, the way you act and the things you say will make a difference.

6. The truth doesn't have to answer the question.

7. The high road is more challenging and more rewarding.

8. Let the toasters go.

9. Never involve the kids.

10. Be careful about playing the victim.

11. It's going to be expensive!

Custody battles are full of emotion and energy. You need to be prepared for moments of doubt, sadness, delusion, excitement, fear, enthusiasm, remorse, joy and euphoria. The more you prepare in advance, the better equipped you will be to deal with your emotions when reality strikes.

I'm Bruce Wallace, the Custody Coach.

I'm here to help you help your child.

THE END

NOTES

APPENDIX

GETTING YOUR SWOT THOUGHTS TOGETHER

Remember, a SWOT Analysis is divided into personal/internal/controllable factors (Strengths and Weaknesses) and external/uncontrollable factors (Opportunities and Threats). You want to leverage the Strengths and Opportunities and avert the Weaknesses and Threats of your case.

On the following pages, make a list of the Strengths, Weaknesses, Opportunities and Threats of your case. This is the first step to properly preparing your personalized SWOT. Be brutally honest. The more you reveal and understand about

your case the better you'll be able to anticipate the

strategies and tactics of your opponent.

Strengths:

1.

2.

3.

4.

5.

6.

7.

8.

9.

10.

NOTES

Weaknesses:

1.

2.

3.

4.

5.

6.

7.

8.

9.

10.

NOTES

<u>O</u>pportunities:

1.

2.

3.

4.

5.

6.

7.

8.

9.

10.

NOTES

Threats:

1.

2.

3.

4.

5.

6.

7.

8.

9.

10.

NOTES

ABOUT THE AUTHOR

Bruce Wallace
Founder & Head Coach
Custody Coaching, LLC

My primary objective is helping you make sure the results of your custody battle are in the best interests of your children and the families of both parents. I'm not an attorney or a professional counselor. I won't be giving you legal or psychological advice. So, you're probably wondering what qualifies me to help you prepare for your divorce and/or custody battle. It comes down to this.

I went into my second custody battle for my six-year-old daughter at the age of 60, previously divorced three times, past due over $50,000 in alimony and owing my ex-spouse a $60,000 judgement for attorney's fees. My ex and the judge assigned to my case were both single working moms. The odds of winning my case were clearly stacked against me. There's no way I should have won my custody battle. But, I did!

I'm confident coming out on top in a divorce and/or custody battle requires the same skills and expertise you need to win a boardroom presentation. You must understand your opponent's current position, uncover their needs, disrupt their mindset, provide reasonable solutions, overcome objections and convince your opponent that your solution(s) are in everyone's best interest. If you're not approaching your custody battle with this skillset, you're leaving yourself at a clear disadvantage.

I graduated Baylor University and have enjoyed a professional marketing and distribution career my entire life. My most recent executive position was Senior Vice President and Chief Marketing Officer for a large life insurance company. I've successfully won many multi-million-dollar boardroom presentations. With this in mind, my professional experience puts me in a unique position to determine the necessary preparation, strategies and tactics you'll need to be successful.

I've been through two very difficult, high-conflict divorces involving my children. I lost custody in my first battle, learned from my mistakes and won custody the second time around. You can learn from my mistakes, leverage my professional background and dramatically improve your chances for winning.

I'd like to help you. You'll find I'm a good listener and I'm easy to get to know. I'll be open and transparent regarding my divorces and custody battles. You'll be surprised to learn that in one way or another I've likely experienced the same things as you.

Let's get together if you want to learn more about my experiences and determine if there's more you can do to better prepare for battle. An Introductory Meeting with me is complementary;

so, you've got nothing to lose. Simply go to: www.CustodyCoaching.com/book-online. I look forward to visiting with you.

Made in the USA
Monee, IL
22 May 2022